Performing Artist Series

FRANZ SCHUBERT
Piano Works

Edited by Joseph Banowetz

AF822314

DEDICATION

This volume is dedicated to Iain B. McKay,
ever loyal friend and mentor

Director of Keyboard Publications: GAIL LEW
Project Manager: DALE TUCKER
Production Coordinator: KARL BORK
Art Design: LISA GREENE MANE

CONTENTS

ABOUT THE EDITOR

JOSEPH BANOWETZ has been described in *Fanfare Record Review* (U.S.) as "a giant among keyboard artists of our time," and by *Russia's News* (Moscow) as "a magnificent virtuoso." He has been heard as recitalist and orchestral soloist on five continents, with guest appearances in recent seasons with such orchestras as the St. Petersburg (formerly the Leningrad) Philharmonic, the New Zealand Symphony (in a twelve-concert national tour), the Prague Radio Symphony, the Moscow State Symphony, the Belarus National Philharmonic of Minsk, the Hong Kong Philharmonic, the Shanghai Symphony, and the Beijing Central Philharmonic.

Banowetz has received international critical acclaim for his series of compact disc recordings for the Marco Polo, Naxos, and Altarus labels. His world-premiere recording of Balakirev works received a German Music Critics' outstanding record of the year award, and his world-premiere recording of Anton Rubinstein's Concertos Nos. 1 and 2 received a similar citation from *Fanfare Record Review* (U.S.). He has recorded twenty-two compact discs including concertos of Tchaikovsky's, Liszt's, and d'Albert's and the world-premiere recordings of all eight of the Anton Rubinstein works for piano and orchestra. Banowetz has recorded with the Slovak State Radio Orchestra, the Czecho-Slovak State Philharmonic, the Budapest Symphony, the Beijing Central Opera Orchestra, and the Hong Kong Philharmonic.

A graduate with a First Prize from the Vienna Academy for Music and Dramatic Arts, Banowetz also studied with Carl Friedberg (a pupil of Clara Schumann's) and Gÿorgy Sándor (a pupil of Béla Bartók's). In addition to his performance and recording activities, he has given lectures and masterclassses at such schools as Juilliard in New York City, the St. Petersburg Conservatory, the Royal College of Music in London, the Beijing Central Conservatory, the Shanghai Conservatory, and the Hong Kong Academy for the Performing Arts.

Banowetz has been invited to serve on many international piano competition juries, these having included the Gina Bachauer International Piano Competition (United States), the Arthur Rubinstein International Piano Master Competition (Israel), the Scottish International Piano Competition (Glasgow), and the PTNA Young Artists Competition (Japan). His award-winning book *The Pianist's Guide to Pedaling* has been printed in five languages. In 1992 Banowetz was presented with the Liszt Medal by the Hungarian Liszt Society in Budapest. Mr. Banowetz is a Steinway artist.

Presently Banowetz is on the Artist Piano Faculty of the University of North Texas.

ABOUT THIS EDITION

Schubert's music remains some of the most beloved by musicians everywhere. This collection attempts to gather together selections that are not only artistically of a high level but also are suitable for the moderately advanced performer. From the elegant *Valses nobles* to the profoundly expressive *Moments musicaux,* Schubert's music both charms and moves the listener. Many of the works in this anthology can serve as a valuable introduction to his warm, lyrical style. Included is background information on each work, as well as suggestions for practice and performance. Also included is a guide to some of the more recent valuable research done on Schubert and his music.

In this edition, Schubert's original markings have been left intact. Very often these are only partially complete, or else may be given for a few measures before the performer is assumed to continue the same patterns. Many of these omissions have been clarified by additions of supplemental markings enclosed in brackets. In some cases, incomplete dynamic indications have been added, these again always being set apart in brackets. Very rarely (as in measure 22 of the *Moment musicale,* No. 4) Schubert has an indication for use of pedal. Both the damper and *una corda* pedals will naturally be needed in much of his piano music and have been added by the editor in modern notation. Editorial suggestions for metronome indications are given in brackets.

Ornamentation is always a controversial issue, with not all authorities agreeing on the same way to perform a given ornament. The editor has tried to make suggestions for various realizations that are based on scholarly research and his practical experience as a performing artist. Schubert lived in a transition period between the classic and romantic eras, at a time when many performance conventions were in a state of flux. It is therefore often difficult to give a dogmatic answer for a given realization of an ornament.

A portrait of Schubert in 1821 by Kupelwieser

About Franz Schubert

Franz Peter Schubert, one of music's greatest lyricists, was born January 31, 1797, in Himmelpfortgrund, a suburb of Vienna. He was the twelfth in a family of 14. Schubert's father ran a boys' school, while his mother was in domestic service. As a boy, Schubert sang in the Imperial Court Choir, at the same time receiving top schooling at the Imperial Royal Seminary. Additional music study was received from Antonio Salieri, the renowned but ill-fated composer who was rumored to have poisoned Mozart. From 1814 to 1816 Schubert served in his father's school as a teaching assistant, often giving as much as nine hours of daily instruction. Finally breaking free from this crushing workload, he began a bohemian life, sharing living quarters with various friends and essentially living from hand to mouth. The only time he spent away from the Vienna area was during the summers of 1818 and 1824, teaching music lessons at the Esterhazy estate in Hungary. Schubert's day-to-day schedule seems to have been spent composing from the early morning hours until about two in the afternoon and then socializing with friends until late in the evening in one or another of Vienna's coffee houses. It seems miraculous that he was able to write the enormous amount of music he did during the brief few years left in his life.

Schubert from many accounts was relatively shy and quiet, although he apparently had dark moods, especially when drinking heavily. He was just five feet tall, and contemporary pictures show him as being dimpled and pudgy, with a snub nose, and sensitive eyes peering from behind thick glasses. His friends nicknamed him Schwammerl, or "little mushroom." Schubert seems to have been a reasonably accomplished pianist, as evidenced by his tirelessly improvising waltzes at parties to accompany the dancing of his friends. He played the violin as well. Word of Schubert's talent spread in Viennese musical circles, and his music was performed at many *Schubertiaden,* private concerts during social evenings when Schubert would be a major musical contributor either as a performer or composer. By 1812 the well-known publishing company Cappi and Diabelli began to print Schubert's music, although they exploited him mercilessly by paying low fees, making alterations in scores without his consent, and usually ignoring his more important works.

Schubert became extremely ill in 1823 with syphilis and was a patient at Vienna's General Hospital. At that time penicillin and similar drugs now taken for granted were unknown. Although he momentarily improved, Schubert's situation made him a fatally marked man, with a total cure being impossible at the time. Yet during the short five years left to him, he continued to write huge quantities of some of the world's greatest music.

Although Beethoven also lived in Vienna, he and Schubert possibly met only as late as March 18, 1827, shortly before Beethoven's death. Unfortunately no details of this (or a rumored earlier meeting in 1822) are known, and the sources of this information are controversial. Eleven days later Schubert was a torch bearer in Beethoven's funeral procession. Schubert's own health continued to deteriorate rapidly. In October of the following year, while visiting his brother Ferdinand, Schubert became ill with typhoid fever and then died November 19, 1828. In his final moments he expressed terrible fears about being buried alive. His grave now lies a short distance from Beethoven's, with an epitaph written by the playwright Franz Grillparzer: "The art of music here entombed a rich possession, but even fairer hopes."

During his short 31-year lifetime, Schubert wrote an incredibly large quantity of music not only for the piano but also for orchestra, chamber music ensemble, and voice. There is an expressiveness in his writing that undoubtedly mirrors the complex emotions contained in his own personality. Especially characteristic is an intense bittersweet quality that has been fittingly described as "smiling through the tears." Schubert's music contains a marvelous sensitivity to harmonic tension and color, with never a hint of cheap technical display or emotional superficiality. There is an extensive amount of music written by him for the piano. While some of the piano sonatas are huge in scope, many of the smaller works are molded after dance forms and reflect the types of pieces that were then popular in Vienna. Like Beethoven's, Schubert's music has a timeless quality that has kept it alive to the present day.

Schubert's father,
Franz Theodor Florin Schubert.
Oil painting by his son,
Karl Schubert.

ABOUT THE DANCE PIECES OF SCHUBERT'S DAY

In Vienna during the first decade of the nineteenth century, the most common dance was still the minuet. But this soon changed, as reflected in a profusion of additional titles such as ecossaise, deutscher tanz (German dance), ländler, valse, galop, and cotillon used by Schubert. It should always be remembered that most of Schubert's dance pieces were improvised for actual dancing and then written down at a later time. Therefore, they should not in general be played at breakneck tempos. The famous Viennese "lift" can be used to excellent effect if done with taste and elegance. To gain this effect, slightly shorten when appropriate the first beat in a valse, ländler, or deutscher tanz while giving the second beat a corresponding bit of additional time. Often the damper pedal can be released on the second beat to help project the rhythm.

Recordings of such conductors as Clemens Krauss, Willi Boskovsky, and Bruno Walter conducting the Vienna Philharmonic in waltzes by Johann Strauss show how to use this important rubato effect.

ABOUT SCHUBERT AND THE SO-CALLED "CHARACTER PIECE"

Schubert wrote many smaller pieces that, along with later works by Schumann, Chopin, Mendelssohn, Brahms, and many others, have been termed "character pieces." Schubert's Impromptus, Moments musicaux, Scherzi, and Marches all fall into this wide category of pieces, many of which have little in common aside from being relatively short and often written with one dominating mood or character. Some of Schubert's most captivating writing can be found in these concise and less imposing musical structures.

Schubert's birthplace, in the Himmelpfortgrund
district of Vienna. Watercolor painting by Franz Kopallik.

Schubert at the age of 17.
Drawing by Moritz von Schwind.

ABOUT THE PIECES IN THIS ANTHOLOGY

ALLEGRETTO IN C MINOR, D. 915:

This lovely untitled composition was written April 27, 1827, in a farewell album for Schubert's friend, the lawyer and amateur singer Ferdinand Walcher, who was leaving for Venice to serve in the Austrian navy. It was not published until 1870. Pay the most careful attention to dropping the dynamics at the ends of slurs and phrases, especially when they come before rests. In the opening section, try to convey the idea of two people speaking, especially when the unison melodic lines trail after each other in measures 9–13. Throughout, there should he a feeling of sad resignation, punctuated only at the bars marked fortissimo by what seems a momentary angry questioning of fate.

TRAUERWALZER, NO. 2, FROM ERSTE WALZER, OPUS 9, D. 365:

The title *Trauerwalzer* can perhaps be best translated as *Mourning Waltz.* It is the second in a set of 36 waltzes written between 1816 and 1821 and exists in several manuscript versions. Even before its publication in 1821, the *Trauerwalzer* became enormously popular with the Viennese public. The name was not given by Schubert, who upon learning of his composition's increasing popularity was reported to have said, "What fool would write a mournful waltz?!" A successful performance of this piece should be expressive, without indulging in mock heart-on-the-sleeve sentimentality and excessive rubati.

Autograph of Schubert's *Trauerwalzer (Mourning Waltz),* Opus 9, No. 2, D. 365. Dated March 14, 1818.

VARIATION IN C MINOR ON A WALTZ BY ANTON DIABELLI, D. 719:

In 1819 Cappi and Diabelli, the prominent Viennese publishers, invited 50 Austrian composers to each contribute a variation on a waltz written by Anton Diabelli. Beethoven produced one of his greatest masterpieces, a huge set of 33 variations, which was published in 1823. The other composers had their single variations printed in an anthology a year later. In addition to Schubert, these composers included the child prodigy Franz Liszt and his teacher Karl Czerny. The actual date of composition for Schubert's variation was 1821. In measures 8–10, Schubert's awkward large chords can be facilitated by redistributions between the hands. Otherwise, break in such a way that the rhythmic flow is not disrupted. Make clear the three-note slurs in measures 1 (with upbeat) and 5 (with upbeat). These should sound different from the two-note slurs found in measures 16–18 and 20–22. Although no tempo marking is found in the original, a successful performance should be both vivacious and lively.

Schubert's *Variations in C minor on a Waltz by Anton Diabelli,* D. 718.
First printed edition by Diabelli and Co., 1824.

MARCH IN E MAJOR, D. 606:

According to a list of Schubert's works made by his brother Ferdinand, the March in E Major was written in 1818, when Schubert was 21 years of age. It was published only after Schubert's death, in 1840. Try to avoid both a harsh tone quality and the temptation to play loudly always, saving a real *fortissimo* only for the passages so marked. The trio section starting in measure 53 should be played entirely without pedal so that the left-hand chords will remain *staccato*.

TWO SCHERZI, IN B-FLAT MAJOR AND D-FLAT MAJOR, D. 593:

Both of these charming pieces were written in November of 1817 yet remained unpublished until 1871. The title Scherzo means literally a "joke." Schubert first used the Trio of the Scherzo in D-flat Major in the minuetto movement of his earlier piano Sonata in E-flat Major, D. 568. In the Scherzo in B-flat Major, some performers prefer to play the short grace notes on the beat. The editor prefers them before the beat, so as to not disrupt the eighth-note rhythm in the melody. Which ever way is preferred, they should be played lightly and rapidly, with a slight "bite" to convey the dissonance with the following eighth note. In both scherzi, be especially cautious in using the pedal. As in much piano music by Haydn, Mozart, and Beethoven, the writing of Schubert always requires the player to be aware not only of the material to be pedaled but also of the writing in other parts, to avoid carelessly obscuring rests and subtle differences in touch indications. Think of the damper pedal as a tool for coloring, not as a lazy way to play legato.

VALSES NOBLES, OPUS 77, D. 969:

First published in January of 1827, this charming group of 12 dances is an excellent example of the kind of dance music Schubert must have improvised for his friends at parties. In a number of these valses, a discreet Viennese "lift" rhythm can be used (see the previous notes under "About Dance Pieces in Schubert's Day"). Liszt composed a marvelous set of nine pieces entitled *Soirées de Vienne (Vienna Evenings),* which are based on a number of Schubert dances. In addition to using the Trauerwalzer (included in the present anthology) in the *Soirée de Vienne,* No. 9, he uses the *Valse noble,* No. 3, in the *Soirée de Vienne,* No. 5, and the *Valses nobles,* Nos. 9 and 10, in the *Soirée de Vienne,* No. 6. Liszt's own pupil, the great pianist Moriz Rosenthal (1862–1946), recorded the *Soirée de Vienne,* No. 6, in 1936. In his performance he uses the Viennese "lift" elegantly.

SIX MOMENTS MUSICAUX, OPUS 94, D. 780:

The *Moments musicaux* are some of Schubert's most personal pieces and have remained favorites of audiences and performers. No. 3 was published in 1823, with the others being possibly written between then and the later publication of the entire series in a two-volume set in 1828. The original title was *Moments musicals,* this probably an invention of the publisher. Now this is usually changed to a more correct French spelling, *Moments musicaux.*

No. 1, Moderato: Although many of Schubert's grace notes should be played on the beat, the editor feels that to do so in measures 1, 9, 12, 13, and 14 and similar later places would disrupt too much the triplet rhythm. In measure 1, make a clear difference between the triplet and dotted eighth-sixteen rhythms. Measures 18–21, carefully make a small diminuendo between each eighth-sixteenth note slurred pair. A relaxed, slight raising of the wrist to lighten the last note of each slur will help accomplish this. In the left-hand broken octaves in measures 59–65, hold each note over so there are no hiccups in the texture as the damper pedal is changed with the right-hand chords.

No. 2, Andantino: Although this lovely piece is meditative in nature, Schubert indicates that a long phrase line should be maintained by giving a tempo indication of Andantino. In the F-sharp minor section starting at measure 18, some performers lightly detach each note marked with a staccato in the left hand. It is helpful to think of these staccatos as pizzicatos on a cello; then use light pedaling to keep the entire texture from being too dry. The following slurred eighths should receive a slight emphasis on the first notes of each slur. Throughout, make careful differences between piano and pianissimo dynamic levels. The forte outburst in measure 56 should sound anguished but not harsh and aggressive.

No. 3, Allegro moderato: Probably the most frequently performed of the set, the third *Moment musicale* has remained a favorite encore piece for many performers. The great Polish pianist Leopold Godowsky (1870–1938) made a witty transcription of it for more advanced pianists. Do not pick a tempo that is too fast, but rather think of this piece as a small march that builds to a climax in measures 19–22 and then recedes into the distance. Pay the most careful attention to the subtle differences in slurring throughout the right-hand part while playing *sempre staccato* in the left hand. Except for the last chord, the editor suggests avoiding the damper pedal entirely.

No. 4, Moderato: Schubert's indication for Moderato should be followed, for too many performers make the opening and closing sections sound like a rapid Czerny etude. Play the right-hand sixteenths legato, the left hand a light staccato, and think in long phrases. The first phrase, for instance, should extend from measures 1 through 8. No pedal should be used until arriving at measure 22, where Schubert indicates a general use of pedal; then again have some pedal beginning in measure 31. The middle section starting at measure 62 can be slightly slower than the outer sections but should not give the impression of being an entirely different tempo. Show the slurs over each opening pair of sixteenths, and do not extend these slurs to the following quarter-note chords. As in the opening section, always think in longer phrases. For instance, measures 62–65 can be thought of as a phrase, which is answered by the following measures 66–69. It would have been easy for Schubert to end this *Moment musicale* on an optimistic D-flat major tonal level. He instead ends very darkly and ominously in C-sharp minor.

No. 5, Allegro vivace: This aggressive and relentless piece reminds me of a demonic chase or ride. To keep from getting technically stiff, make certain the wrist remains flexible in the staccato chords. Avoid the temptation to simply bang the entire way through, but save your loudest tone for the fortissimo passages only. Some editors feel that, through a possible printing error in the first edition, the final repeat should come not in the last measure but at the end of measure 96, with measures 97–111 acting as an epilogue. The performer must decide since Schubert's original manuscript is lost.

No. 6, Allegretto: This lovely *Moment musicale,* with its mood of quietness and its twilight ending in minor, concludes the entire set of *Moments musicaux* with a feeling of profound sadness and resignation. Choose a flowing allegretto tempo that is not pushed yet will allow for a clear projecting of the eight-measure phrases found throughout much of the writing.

A charade game at a Schubertian home. Schubert is seated at the piano. Watercolor painting by Leopold Kupelwieser in 1821.

SUGGESTIONS FOR FURTHER READING

Clive, Peter. *Schubert and His World: A Biographical Dictionary.* Oxford, Clarendon Press, 1997. (A chronicle of the composer's life is followed by more than 300 biographical entries relating to Schubert's friends, business acquaintances, and later musicians associated with his music. The book concludes with an extensive up-to-date bibliography. This is an important supplemental book to accompany any Schubert biography.)

Deutsch, Otto Erich. *The Schubert Thematic Catalogue.* New York, Dover Publications, Inc., 1995. (This contains a thematic index of all of Schubert's music, accompanied by dates of composition and publication, and known locations of Schubert's manuscripts. Since Deutsch's numbering system has been universally adopted, this alone makes his book a must reference work for serious musicians.)

Erickson, Raymond. *Schubert's Vienna.* New Haven and London, Yale University Press, 1997. (This fascinating book is at least as much about early nineteenth-century Vienna, Schubert's home, as it is about the composer himself. Erickson and a distinguished group of contributors give valuable insights into various aspects of Schubert's world, all of which are vital to fully understanding his music.)

Marek, George R. *Schubert.* New York, Viking Penguin, Inc., 1985. (Marek's Schubert is highly readable yet extremely well researched and thorough. This is an excellent "first Schubert biography" for anyone to start with.)

McKay, Elizabeth Norman. *Franz Schubert: A Biography*. Oxford, Clarendom Press, 1996. (In this recent Schubert biography, McKay does not hesitate to examine some of the darker and unsettling aspects of Schubert's life and dispels any lingering images of the naive, innocent Schubert portrayed in such cloying musicals as Sigmund Romberg's *Blossom Time.* Necessary, if not always pleasant, reading for serious musicians.

Weekley, Dallas A. and Nancy Arganbright. *Schubert's Music for Piano Four-Hands: A Comprehensive Guide to Performing and Listening to the Dances, Fantasies, Marches, Polonaises, Sonatas, Variations, and Other Duets.* White Plains, New York, Pro/Am Music Resources, Inc., 1990. (This is a comprehensive examination of Schubert's duet literature both from an historical standpoint and in practical aspects of performance. Schubert's output for piano duet is extensive and important. Weekley and Arganbright comprehensively illuminate this too-often unexplored area of his composing.)

Franz Schubert.
Watercolor painting by
Wilhelm August Rieder
in 1825.

Franz Schubert. Oil painting by Josef Mähler.

ALLEGRETTO IN C MINOR
D. 915

FRANZ SCHUBERT
Edited by JOSEPH BANOWETZ

Track 1

Allegretto [M.M. ♩. = 66-69]

*For pianists with sufficiently large enough hands, the following redistribution will insure a smooth *legato* phrase ending.

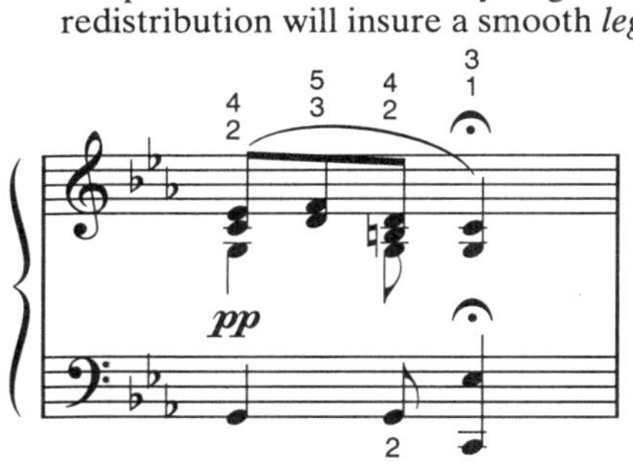

35
fp
pp
[p]
una corda
tre corde
40
45
pp
una corda
49
f
tre corde
53
pp
pp
1.
2.
D.C. al Fine
una corda

MARCH IN E MAJOR
D. 606

FRANZ SCHUBERT
Edited by JOSEPH BANOWETZ

Allegro con brio [M.M. 𝅗𝅥 = 72-76]

17
fz
p
21
ff
25
fz
[p]
29
ff
34
ff

38
fz
fz
42
staccato
fz
46
staccato
49
fz
Fine
53
Trio
[p] legato sempre
l.h.
Basso staccato
[senza Pedale]

56
[più p]
sempre staccato
59
l.h.
[mp]
63
[p]
66
69
fz
fz cresc.
fz

72
fz
ff
fz
75
fz
fz
p
Basso staccato
78
Marcia Da Capo al Fine
81
[sempre staccato]

VARIATION IN C MINOR ON A WALTZ BY ANTON DIABELLI

D. 719

FRANZ SCHUBERT
Edited by JOSEPH BANOWETZ

Track 3

***[Allegro vivace M.M. ♩= 168-176]**

*Schubert gives no tempo indication.

17
pp
20
24
28
r.h.

SCHERZO No. 1 IN B-FLAT MAJOR
D. 593

FRANZ SCHUBERT
Edited by JOSEPH BANOWETZ

*Play the small notes very lightly and rapidly before the beat. To play them on the beat would disturb the flow of the eighth-note rhythm.

14
p
17
fp
[p]
[fp]
pp
[una corda]
21
[sempre pp]
24
l.h.
27
l.h.
p
[cresc.]
[tre corde]

*The following redistribution will greatly facilitate this passage.

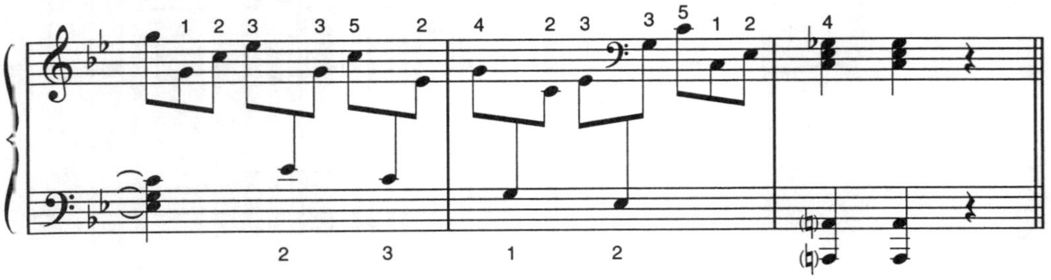

47
[ff]
[p]
Fine
Trio
51
legato
p
55
60

Scherzo da Capo

SCHERZO No. 2 IN D-FLAT MAJOR
D. 593

FRANZ SCHUBERT
Edited by JOSEPH BANOWETZ

Track 5

Allegro moderato [M.M. ♩= 132-138]

*The turn sounds less square if begun immediately after the third beat. The Editor prefers to play an E-sharp, although this is not indicated by a sharp being placed underneath the turn sign.

**Realization:

32
dim.
37
ff [subito]
40
fp
fp
45
p
49
ff
[senza dim.]
l.h.
fp

*The tempo of the *Trio* can be slightly more relaxed.

*The editor offers alternate fingerings in measures 76 and 77.

TRAUERWALZER (MOURNING WALTZ)

Op. 9, No. 2, D. 365

FRANZ SCHUBERT
Edited by JOSEPH BANOWETZ

*Schubert gives no tempo indication.

VALSES NOBLES
Opus 77, D. 969

Track 7

FRANZ SCHUBERT
Edited by JOSEPH BANOWETZ

* [M.M. ♩ = 152-160]

*Schubert gives no suggestions for tempi in any of the *Waltzes.* The Editor's proposed tempo indication fits all of the *Waltzes.* If a basic tempo (with minor fluctuations according to mood) is maintained for all the *Waltzes,* this acts as a strong unifying factor when the entire set is performed.

Track
8
[simile]
2
4
9
14
1.
2.

Track
9
3
p
6
[>]
cresc.
11
p
16
decresc.
pp

21
p
cresc.
[>]
26
[>]
[mf]
p
30
decresc.
pp
34
[mp]
39
dim.

43
ff
47
[>]
51
[f]
cresc.
55
8va
[ff]

*The performer may choose to release the pedal on each second beat, while in the left hand playing a slight Viennese "lift" rhythm. See the discussion of this rhythm in the *Preface* section entitled *About the Dance Pieces of Schubert's Day.*

Track
11
5
f
fz
6
p
13
[fz]
19
26

Track 12
6
p
[l.h. sempre stacc.]
[senza pedale]
4
9
[mp]
[p]
13

Track
13
7
ff
fz
4
8va
9
14
p
20
[ff]

*Schubert probably intended chords to be rolled throughout.

Track 15

19
fz
p
[subito]
cresc.
24
f
ff
28
fz
fz
fz
33
fz
fz

*Schubert's indication for *legato* refers to the right hand. The left hand should remain a light *staccato* throughout, except for the longer chords in measures 8 and 16.

Track
17
11
fp
5
[cresc.]
9
f
13
ff

12

8va
(8va)
19
f
(8va)
24
28
ff
32
8va

MOMENT MUSICALE No. 1

Opus 94, D. 780

Track 19

FRANZ SCHUBERT
Edited by JOSEPH BANOWETZ

Moderato [M.M. ♩ = 104-108]

15
fz
fz
fz
fz
18
p
decresc.
pp
21
24
pp
27
cresc.
fp

30
p
33
36
pp
40
[simile]
43
cresc.

46
f
49
l.h.
pp
[subito]
[una corda]
p
[tre corde]
52
55
58
pp

61
[simile]
64
dim.
[ppp]
[una corda]
p
[tre corde]
68
pp
72
cresc.
fp
p
76
f

80
fz
fz
fz
fz
83
1
decresc.
pp
87
92
pp
[cresc.]
fp

MOMENT MUSICALE No. 2
Opus 94, D. 780

FRANZ SCHUBERT
Edited by JOSEPH BANOWETZ

11
[tre corde]
14
[p]
17
[simile]
20
[l.h. simile]
23
cresc.

26
[mp]
29
p
32
35
p

38
[fp]
41
pp
[una corda]
44
cresc.
[tre corde]
47
pp
50

53
[>]
56
f
58
61
p
64
pp
p
[una corda]
[tre corde]

67
70
pp
[una corda]
73
[𝄒]
pp
76
[fp]

79
pp
[una corda]
f
[tre corde]
p
82
pp
[una corda]
85
88
[ppp]

MOMENT MUSICALE No. 3

Opus 94, D. 780

FRANZ SCHUBERT
Edited by JOSEPH BANOWETZ

Track 21

Allegro moderato [M.M. ♩ = 92-96]

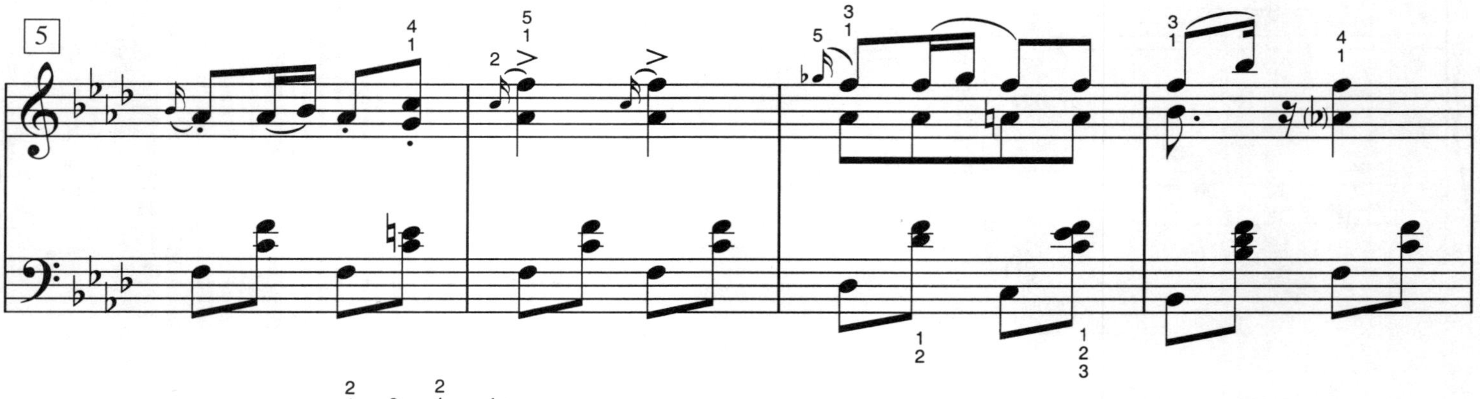

*The small notes are controversial, with some performers playing them before the beat, others on the beat. Whichever way is chosen, they should be rapid, and done in such a way so as to give a certain "bite" to the note that follows. The following realizations are favored by the Editor. Each of these can be applied to similar places found later in the piece.

**Here is another fingering possibility, which is favored by the Editor:

13
17
f
21
p
25
pp
29

33
l.h.
37
ppp
[una corda]
41
[mp]
dim.
[tre corde]
45
dim.
[sempre dim.]
50
[poco rit.]
[ppp]

MOMENT MUSICALE No. 4

Opus 94, D. 780

FRANZ SCHUBERT
Edited by JOSEPH BANOWETZ

*The Ped. indication simply indicates a general use of pedal. Although the similar passages beginning in measures 52, 124 and 154 do not have such an indication, pedal should undoubtedly be used.

35
39
pp
43
47
51
pp

*In the first edition the articulation indications are both incomplete and inconsistent. Most performers will prefer to play ♬ ♩‿♪ rather than the less idiomatic and lilting ♬‿♩‿♪ articulated grouping.

*In the first printed edition there is no natural before the F. In bar 80 a flat is printed before the F in the right hand. Undoubtedly F natural was intended in both measures 78 and 80.

94
99
[simile]
[>]
cresc.
[>]
1.
2.
pp [subito] mf
pp
[subito]
[Tempo I]
103
p
legato
[staccato]
107
[simile]
111

115
118
121
pp
125
128

132
f
136
139
pp
143
147

150
153
pp
157
161
164
Coda
ppp
ritard.
[una corda]

MOMENT MUSICALE No. 5

Opus 94, D. 780

FRANZ SCHUBERT
Edited by JOSEPH BANOWETZ

*Schubert often indicated patterns of articulation for only a few measures, then assumed the performer would continue these patterns in similar passages.

25
fz
p
fz
p
31
fz
p
fz
pp
37
42
[simile]
47
cresc.

53
58
f
ff
63
ff
p
ff
p
l.h.
69
cresc.
75
r.h.
f
[simile]
p

81
[fz]
[fz] cresc.
[fz]
87
[fz]
ff
93
fz
p
99
ff
p
105
ff
p
ff
p
ff

MOMENT MUSICALE No. 6
Opus 94, D. 780

FRANZ SCHUBERT
Edited by JOSEPH BANOWETZ

Track 24

Allegretto [M.M. ♩= 120-126]

22
pp
28
mf
32
fp
pp
37
fp
pp
41
cresc.

46
p
f
p
52
pp
57
f [p]
[f]
62
ff
67
p
fp

72
Trio
78
82
86
91

94
98
pp
102
107
111
Allegretto D.C.